T0288084

DISAPPEARING
ACTS

Charles
Borkhuis

chax
2014

Cover photo by Charles Borkhuis, "Corrupted Pixels-419"

ISBN 978-0-9894316-8-2

Chax Press
411 N 7th Ave Ste 103
Tucson AZ 85705-8388
USA

Printed and Bound in USA

To my parents
Anne and Edward Borkhuis

Acknowledgments

The author gratefully acknowledges the following publications
in which poems from *Disappearing Acts* first appeared:

Hypnogogic Sonnets – Red Dust
    (chapbook editor: Joanna Gunderson)
Dinner with Franz – Meeting Eyes Bindery/Poetry New York
    (chapbook editor: Tod Thilleman
Department of Missing Persons 1, 2 – Boog Reader 2
    (editor: David Kirschenbaum/Rodrigo Toscano)
Spasm – 2nd Avenue Poetry
    (editor: Paolo Javier/Alan Clinton
Hesitation at the Threshold – Eoagh 8
    (editor: Tim Trace Peterson)
Objects Release Their Stare – Big Bridge 15
    (editor: Adam Cornford)
Only in Metaphor May We Speak – Otoliths 25, Autumn
    (editor: Mark Young)
Trace Elements – Talisman 41
    (editor: Ed Foster)
Department of Missing Persons 3-6 – Marsh Hawk Review,
    Spring 2013 (editor: Tom Fink)
Echoes Drawn upon a Point – Calibanonline 14
    (editor: Lawrence R. Smith)

Also by Charles Borkhuis

Poetry ...
Afterimage (Chax Press, 2006)
Savoir Fear (Meeting Eyes Bindery/Spuyten Duyvil, 2003)
Alpha Ruins (Bucknell University Press, 2000)
Dinner with Franz (Meeting Eyes Bindery, 1998)
Proximity (Stolen Arrows) Sink Press, 1994
Hypnogogic Sonnets (Red Dust, 1992)

Poetry Anthologies ...
Boog Reader 2: An Anthology of NYC Poetry (Boog, 2008)
Walt Whitman Hom(m)age (Turtle Point Press, 2005)
An Avec Sampler #2 (Avec, 1998)
Primary Trouble (Talisman House, 1996)
Writing from the New Coast (Presentation) (o.blek 12, 1993)
Writing from the New Coast (Technique) (o.blek 12, 1993)

Poetics ...
*We Who Love to Be Astonished: Experimental Women's Writing and
Performance Poetics* (University of Alabama Press, 2002*)*
> *Im.age . . . Dis.solve: The Linguistic Image in the Critical
> Lyric of Norma Cole and Ann Lauterbach (essay)*
Telling It Slant: Avant-garde Poetics of the 1990s (University of
Alabama Press, 2000)
> *Writing from Inside Language: Late Surrealism and Textual
> Poetry in France and the United States (essay)*

Translation ...
New Exercises by Franck André Jamme, from the French
(Wave Books, 2008)

Theater ...
Stage This: Vol. 3 (Stage This Press, 2009)
> *Present Tense (play)*
The Sound of Fear Clapping (Obscure Press, 2003) *(play)*
Mouth of Shadows (Spuyten Duyvil, 2000)
> *Hamlet's Ghosts Perform Hamlet (play)*
> *Sunspots (play)*
Sunspots (Company One Press, 1993) *(play)*
Theater Ex: Journal (Theater Ex Press, 1986-1988), editor
Poets' Theater (Ailanthus Press, 1981)
> *Phantom Limbs (play)*

Radio ...
Plays produced for National Public Radio (www.pennsound)
Foreign Bodies (Exit 3 Productions, WBGO, 2003)
The Sound of Fear Clapping (The Radio Stage, WNYC, 1995)

DISAPPEARING ACTS

DEAD RECKONING I

Department of Missing Persons

1

to each his own double
loitering inside the ruins

body echo to go
so easy to be displaced

playback to a former self astride
his wife's galloping flanks while thinking

of a future self who never quite arrives
(I am speaking to you in the present

which is already a memory)
in this two-way mirror of sky and bone

someone in my past is listening in
wondering if he's hearing voices

2

whispers through the static ...
which of you insists on speaking for me

an actor points to a seagull
screeching over choppy waves

later a voice on his answering machine
announces the end of a torrid but

ultimately meaningless love affair
listen closer ... sonic waves

of someone in the womb still kicking
close your eyes ... you are standing

between the one already dead
and the one not yet born

3

all this will pass in the time
it takes to tie my shoe

or it will fester for a lifetime
whichever comes first

peek inside the gold ring
and find a ghost of lead filings

under a blue flame still dancing
nothing is ever over

the eternal return has already arrived
whoever was not born sufficiently

will not die definitively
but hover in the subjunctive indefinitely

4

there's no more going around it
or through it making faces

won't help once it has you
flattened thinner than a hair

and reversed every gesture
every smile runs backwards

you've been caught in a web
of haunted images but the spider

is long gone in fact so are you
you're not a reflection

you're a person who just can't see
his face in the glass anymore

5

place a hand on the head of the child
what does his skull see

rows of trees bending at the knees
a green lion slowly eating the sun

in one scenario he's his father's favorite
in another he's dishonored and disowned

in one version he's the author of too many books
in another he's a beggar with too few limbs

one moment an intrepid world traveler
the next the man who never left his room

in still another only one world is real
and the others just soap bubbles that pop

6

words exchanged between the one
who has kicked the bucket

and the other
who is still kicking

or the reverse
for surely one thing follows another

forever in order
the numbers fall forth

so one must die
before one is born

or the reverse
whichever comes first

HYPNOGOGIC SONNETS

1

analog sky
second skin (tingling)
distance whipped

by syllables in deep recline
the turning
of things toward their sound

in thought
(grasping and releasing)
where once an egg

weightless
the body buried alive
behind a wall of words

scratches and murmurs
memory and static

2

when first seen
(correction) lettered sleep
moving the pen

fever-child on the ceiling
body in bed
flying over the forest

four men in wolves' clothing
bound through a clearing
leaving bones and silver tails

in a corner of his room
(windy feet)
snow prints collect across the page

he will write
of a howling in the grain

3

where there was a wall
language slash window
dusk climbs the embankment

(glassy peaks)
the swirl of negative fields
number november

thin streams through the trees
finger pine thick
memories ferreting

holes in stumps and logs
a scroll of small stones
unrolls from a rabbit's skull

a screech scatters the clocks
(soon forgotten)

4

in the afterimage
a suffix of suns
behind closed lids

and this shining suit that walks
through a field of marked stones
volumes tilted

a jar (stolen light)
pulling out the steps
word over word in the dark

the act of appearing
in the beam of a flashlight
wire-crossings (her driven flesh)

figures in the lines
(distractions) bleed into years older

5

as if
written with a map
in mind (decoding distance)

walking into speech
the road disappears
in branching digressions

sound (the holding)
a spiral shadow
leaks from the pen

"just for being"
that face in the rocks
those stretch marks on the sheets

broken awareness
(caress) absence in language

6

lights out
on gray matter
descending

through the sentence
via nervous system
voiceover

treetops and falling
leaves in newspapers
(on screen) swimming

through targeted
flight patterns
wordspan and after

the inevitable seed to suck
the last moments to mean

7

(takes a tumble)
as if on stilts
what he's made of

flows freely
the physical outcroppings
of an inner burial site

under the neighborhood
shopping mall
who is where

when an image replaces
being and the bones
are picked clean

talking sun
strapped to the minute hand

8

each station of sound (inhale)
a state
the long arm of the word

reaching out of itself
the bird on the branch is a quill
the then uninterrupted

sound of when
as lying in wait (inverted mystery)
writing through blue

wings and feathers
the darting beak
the nervous eye

flies away and returns
to the nest in his arm

9

as if (alive)
walking up asleep
inclined over the features

of his face wilted "I"s
drooping into childhood "e"s
mirror and counting

black pronoun on the frozen lake
where the foot stops
white between words

gently pulling an arm out of a leg
leaning against
an upper case "I"

he notices his body has become
a form of writing

10

down by yes
in pale slumber
a fissure in the skull

(invisible when awake)
the white road
where the house is worn

as a winter coat
the narrowing dusk
and wounded when

who was it walked
past the slender gate
behind the family circle

a luminous corpse
retractable as sand

11

an awkward "now"
falling in among the oaks
book of false endings

always in the middle when
a russet maple
splits the sun's radiance

sudden visitation in the mouth
seeds try to confess
while being chewed

fossils in the grain
sequential frames of a man
cutting through the trees

dark branches growing
from his head

12

aphasia window
reentering with a few
phrases from the static

a tiny piece of ice floating in water
writing sustained by mistakes
widens the aperture

lone measure
gravity at the second's detonation
backwater skies

night multiplied by its sides
the molting sentence
slithers through fallen leaves

dark before twin rivers
(live and forget)

13

crosshatched by thorns
(another) dead rabbit in the thicket
picked clean as each

the next cry drawn
featureless
loosened from the page

brushed off or blown free
cracking twigs underfoot
the eyes are the first to go

ghosts in the grass
an ocean of bones
below the surface of the hill

imprint of the erased drawing
(still in the paper)

14

rosy wound (detachable in sleep)
the mouth floating
beside branches and pine needles

a numbness sinks
through the bed in stages
a flashlight searching the woods

two silver wolves bead
together in the folds of a leaf
forming ink

awake in dreamskin
a slow shadow over farm and forest
flight as thought tracing

the body's outline (connected to the pen
by a thread)

DEAD RECKONING II

Only in Metaphor May We Meet

1

a woman the size of an ant
is slowly climbing up my right toe

magnified 50x her eyes appear angry
have I changed that much or has she

turn to the next heat-seeking headline
"door-to-door combat at nursing home"

"bomb found inside talking doll"
"land mine awakens under child's foot"

"greenland swallowed by the sea"
the tiny woman has just poked a hole

through the obituary page
and is crawling up my inner thigh

2

lost on a train of thought
I am speeding back to mother

spying me in the mirror's eye
"you'd never do anything to make me

ashamed of you would you"
the alarm clock keeps ringing

in the suitcase overhead
the passengers signal me to open it

turn off the alarm for god's sake
but I won't it's presence is needed

to repeat this moment indefinitely
as a reminder of its passing

3

who is alive and who is not
try matching words to what moves

the living dead dream too
of a life outside the silent bell

that keeps us walking in place
that keeps the stairs

from crumbling under our feet
and the stars from falling

into a puddle in our laps
keep that blissful little smile

from smearing across your winning face
and your breath from sticking to your ribs

4

don't talk to me
of the lower body beast

material subjugation of the soul
by the sex organs

little more than kissing cousins
to the loquacious arsehole

speak rather of the body
possessed by the praying

mantis of the soul the history
of divine persecution in the name

of the idea that shall set you free
but all in good time all in good time

5

no one there when I look . . .
but turn away and they're back

vacant stare from a seeing-eye dog
walking my shadow across a stone wall

the crossing guard blows an icy blast
and the world screeches inches from my shoe

school children freeze into position
as a thought-bubble floats above my head

"maybe we never truly touch
and in love remain unknown"

a cat crossing at the green smiles back
"only in metaphor may we meet"

6

enter where the words end
slow static in ghost letters

the number knows your name
but is bound to silence

identity's inability to connect the dots
too much air between thoughts

dashed upon the blades of waves
the chromosomal alphabet

gone in a glance you drop off
the dozing face of the earth

and appear the day before you arrive
leaving no breath upon the glass

DINNER WITH FRANZ

*The messiah will come only when he
is no longer necessary; he will come
only on the day after his arrival.*

— Franz Kafka

his body as a disappearing act

false sky inside a room
of changing dimensions

a burrow or castle
with outlining districts

where the rhizomes roam

where the stitches ... open

onto an abyss between dinner

and dissolution ...

as if the street

                              had entered his room
                        and woken him in a moment of

                    transgression

turn a table rising

a trick or trace

two little girls giggle
four eight a hundred hands

reaching through

lines of writing

the slats of the cage
where his animal's voice

is almost human

the hands of the father

folded like napkins in prayer

carving the carcass

lowering the gavel

seen in one motion

needles of the machine
inscribing the same ... sentence

across k's flesh

the apple

thrown by the father
that sticks … in his back

the first word
    in the garden

the first step denied
by an infinity of half-steps

between dreaming and waking

between zero and one

an endless ellipses

displaces an empty center …

a segmented

bureaucratic

body

of independent

diachronic

parts

rolls over in sleep

only to wake

as a giant insect

with middleclass table manners

a child is nourished on an infinitesimal crumb …

      a case continues

           through an error
           in the books
           a slip-up
           in the endless
           procession
           of injury claims

   at dinner a declaration

    a father's pious pragmatism

    between courses

the snapping of small bones

the familiar stories
falling from the knives and forks

the surveyor watches

the partitioned plot
become a maze of shifting surfaces

guarded entrances and exits
traversed by a trickle of

maids and

attendants

typists

counselors

millionaires and

whores

circulating through the gates

and contiguous rooms

of justice

the touch of the web-fingered woman
closes his eyes

the kiss of the seamstress
behind the scenes

the sound of her whirring needles
nearing his cheek ...

aborted seductions
leading to further

accusations

investigations

interrogations

entrapments

sweet disclosures

the keys keep turning in the locks

each story ends

with an ostensible acquittal

followed by another arrest

with new paragraphs and chapters

to be written until a new

acquittal is obtained

followed by a new arrest …

the country doctor

sets out across the frozen tundra

bringing the wound
with him in a black bag

his faltering omnipotence

the shit on his shoes
growing maggots

back in the office ...

the putrefying air ...

the insect in the corner ...

the mole in his burrow ...

the panther in his cage ...

the ape at the academy ...

awakened upon the shores

    of an unbearable   felicity

        her frigid

sensuality

    mirrored
    in the incestuous

             neck of his sister ...

the women are connected
    by drops of blood

    which his thirsty body

    cannot drink

letters written never to be

opened

parables carried by a messenger

who is just now

winding through the corridors

and anterooms along the outer circles ...

but who will never arrive

who will remain forever

as if he has not yet

begun

father crunches   numbers

      while picking meat from his teeth

          the heads
          of mother and sister
       are bowed

whispering under their breath …

     franz closes his eyes

     and places his head

       upon the plate

lives go by unnoticed

like crumbs on the table

as if exiled by birth

the body as the site

of dislocations

each beginning starts and ends in the middle

writes the one who never leaves

not to transcend

but become one with
the materials

      he will be the paper in the machine

      the rock into which

      prometheus is melded

beginning and end

        erased

        by inertia and forgetfulness

        blockage and reversal

the hare will never overtake the tortoise

the promise will never leave

the judgment will never arrive

the body is pressed

into printer's ink

only the book remains
but even that is too much

instructions to herr brod

burn the manuscripts posthumously

uncertain to the end

if the solitary

messenger

from a faraway province

ever traversed the distance necessary

to light the first match …

DEAD RECKONING III

Hesitation at the Threshold

1

dreamt I was still alive
but woke up dead

replaceable heads
might explain us in a pinch

or was it a parallel planet earth
where my lips began to graze

upon your moist greenery
and I returned to live inside you

love's little secrets under a milky purr
impossible to detect precisely

where my body stopped
and yours started

2

moving again are we so
one body to another one thought

to another or the illusion thereof
"time for love" I said

words rocking in their echoes
settle back into their shells

like trains sideling next to each other
so one may roll slightly west

or the other east in sleep
am I in my own train moving

or you in yours or both together
bride and groom forever or neither

3

precarious birth between the acts
curtains rising and falling

as eyelids upon a great expanse
divided by the illusion of a first step

characters in reflection dream
of leaving the mirror's double

but find themselves stuck
in flesh or glass as in time itself

fixed to the present where the tenses
fall into each other's arms

and oceans crash face first
into a silent *now*

4

another cruise on the hot seat of the human heart
o love what ails me o iceberg wilderness

feelings from another century unload their cargo
onto my sunken chest enough pain and humiliation

to sink ten titanics in a row and still not know
years later what any of it means

except no one's above those teary
soap opera eyes but when this play dough world

is finally finished with us and truth is no more
than a dented can of bug spray

on a despoiled shore love will still wash up
on my worn out loafers looking for a bone

5

there was a time when touch
might have meant the world

(whose touch what world)
comes a time when distance must supply

the missing intimacy a time when absence
tastes sweet as mother's milk

safe in the space unspoken
someone hides inside me now

someone wears me like a mask
so he may tell a crooked truth

while I lie naked upon white pebbled sand
"matter" light said "casts a ghostly shadow"

6

presence at the folds
neither foreign nor familiar

but intimate disembodied awareness
inhabiting granular relations

between an insect's feelers
and the sun

life in death or the reverse
the void opens

before and after each step
breathing in and out of things

that were never this way or that
but changed in recognition

SPASM

shock the therapy back to the spark then jump

the silent word-flicker between trees but the

keepers are door-wise to the narrow now they

can bird cage fingers off a shadow now I

watched your dark flame leaving in a truck we

were so much left luggage then I might still

hands in pockets freeze I might mad boy play

me dumb take me back upon the road forest

bridge me up again thrashing see the jackknife

trout mid-streaming mute inside the man so

stone's throw from the moon I might just spit

wake me hands shaking from this place I can't keep words to things anymore so objects pass in fever I can't speak to the keepers when I thrust a glowing arm through my shadow when I bang the floor with a boot and roll inside the words I can only shake an empty head stare at the nothing in their eyes stand motionless sun-captured tree so they will never know the circuitry secret sky code lips aflame so I may eat the sun a trick but thought can ignite a bud inside the skull blossom a little voice ago *who's there* my silent twin curls his back against the wall and hangs on every word

I know you're there on the tongue repeat no sound to tie the thread between us *troubled mind* they said and I fell backwards fit to floor to think spasm word-lock bite to hold on fish flapping tail to sky snap upwards bending over houses shadow of an eye over little people looking shoe-ward tiny insect cars I float feather across paper skies while you squat in the bone cage they call out a name I've scribbled in the dirt but they can't read me

just call them *depersonalization attacks* so
needle to dark rivers flow while the dead keep
growing hair I've heard the keepers laugh in
the corridor before lights out heard them in the
storage room sawing off patient's limbs I've
been in the closet with the broom-men I've
tapped days off the wall until the word *fig* fell
from a tree and bounced between stones
a ghost dog brought it to me jawbone of a
loquacious relative I have little doubt but so
bright in this light the peaks of mountains stare

nomadic phrases flit branch to forehead like
plucked strings but lonely few hear the call yet
all know it lie next to it dream the day
backwards to keep close to its echo sleep in
stone under the flying wheel when the curtain
rises someone turns me in like a bad bill I'm
not one of them I walk the shadow stem I ray
the farmer in his field I step in and out of
passing eyes never let the mirror see my face
stay inside the skull-tipped tongue the song of
my head wandering south the flutter of a bird
over closed lids the mouth opens like a jewel

residing in this body you may be punished
while a dark coat of wings fans across my
shoulders crank me up through the propeller-
headed sky to soar in spiral gusts hawk arcing
higher hanging off the edge of the world in a
flap and drift under the silent flame before they
yank the rope between my legs and I scrape
through clouds to splashdown under waves
pull me back on a hook across the ocean floor
to this inside the room to watch them burn the
wings out back and lock the door *never again*
they said *take your meds and straight to bed*

we've learned to write backwards on a wall
mirror a moment that turns back and forth in
time we've learned to play dead before the
statues the keeper touches us further away
through a tunnel of hands you remain in your
body when what happens is not me though
we are the same I escape from the chair
placeholder to the number I throw myself into
the empty I climb inside the mute size of things
I walk into my outline I disappear inside the
keeper's brain burrow deeper there until one
night he hears my voice as if it were his own

DEAD RECKONING IV

Echoes Drawn upon a Point

1

why this bridge this stone
just to hear a plunk in time

I was swallowed by a wave
for speaking out of turn

jumped branch to branch
in widening detours and digressions

talked to a quiver in the arm a running eye
a knock at the knees a humming in the head

who hears the ear in my ear who lives
on the twitch of a lip takes a microphone

into the forest records the serious
chewing under every leaf

2

burrowing through a dark tumble
when a voice whispers "she is waiting"

look up to see your multiples leading separate
but equal lives one falls off the end of a bench

and another takes his place you are
in an audience watching yourself acting

in your own play but your ghost is pissed
you failed to write the play he wanted

your eyes open on a blinking train
racing through a damp narrow tunnel

shake the sleeping woman next to you till
you're blue in the face but she won't wake up

3

and when you have left the room
who has gone

and when you have pivoted slyly
down the hole

who is still with me
caught again misbehaving

as if thought could lean
against the shoulder of a chair

and curl inside the fleshy pulp
of wood spinning in the mind

neither yours nor mine but subjectivity
sans subject traveling the open circuit

4

arthritic tick in reason's bones
or just one trick knee that kicks out

against injustice whereas the educated other
may simply turn and walk away

but then morality was never linked to knowledge
there's an argument there somewhere

I just can't find the thread
though you never know

when a phantom phrase may turn
a page without warning

igniting a drowsy ember under the ribs
don't give up the ghost

5

normally the table doesn't answer
to its name words just bounce

off its blank surface mirror-bent
back to the speaker and his reflection

yet a verbal spell may dwell in the call
and response of a small pink rubber ball

jumping off the wall as if being led
by a child's hand into *objectland*

as if a misheard word had entered accidentally
through a momentary crack in the wall

"let me in" I said as your eyelids fluttered
over a page of choppy waves

6

photo of my face reflected on a shiny
black dinner plate other lifetimes

tap me on the shoulder no doubt
an incomplete separation at birth

so in death remain on call
as if finality were a lost cause

as if I never left the dinner table
and it were only possible

to relive events
to act as if all this were a surprise

in other words to pretend to live
and make a show of it

TRACE ELEMENTS

It is not necessary to live;
it is necessary to travel.

— William S. Burroughs

1

little tremble
sit beside me

in the vast and cloistered

in the veiled word
angling under flesh

whose flesh

might wriggle off the hook
and crawl back to its hole
inside the labyrinthine ear

what I thought I'd heard
in the shutter-clap and worn hinge-rattle
come to finger the insatiable

what the cat dragged in

that I might try in vain
to explain the universe
to a dying vole

look here
the tall grasses

there the convulsive sun
hanging from a branch

2

explain till you have explained away
all explanation

swept the subject under the rug
except for the silence
between things

deafening to the point
of exhaustion
eliciting another

poorly chosen not that
no conclusion but correction
steeped upon correction

what heart could stop
uncertainty by simply

ceasing to beat

3

fall forward
in a moment's suspension

have we ever moved
from this patch of dirt

a twitch in time where lies the rub
o distant learner
double-agent in the crawlspace
under the tongue

click a code
so the words know
which self is knocking at the door
and which is burrowing
through the earth

at the limits of control
one goes
the other stays

as if nothing had happened
in the exchange
of heads

4

take this hand
the one you cannot read

stations of the sentence
where the noun prostrates itself
before the verb
for deeper clarification

intimate knowledge
of the imaginary
upon a branch breaks
in a far-off womb

progeny further exposed
as the second hand splits
and the forked fragment
wriggles both ways

those who dwell in fact
may eventually hear
evening steps fill the room
falling into a childish downpour

these feet from nowhere
climbing over my head
and shoulders as the doorknob

turns to speak

5

let's say a keyhole in sleep
a silhouette adrift dark skirt
in a bell ringing over distant hills
and branching brain away

old skeleton-moon on your right
mouth agape calling flies home

once animal in the hole
with the others
blind to suck
a little light and tremble

words caked in spittle
stir the day
quicksand the night

I only need a few to coax
a little life from this chronic
"yes" and "no"

correction
to shake some space between the bones
to dead-awaken

these stars
this sand

reversible at a moment's notice

6

static in whose ecstasy
invites the chaos in

when metaphors collide
I see sparks from a distant alphabet
come crawling
infant on my tongue

a facial tick
keeps time to every syllable

the marked one
picked up and put down

the back of the wind
on a fence climbing

the stone in the meadow
picked up and put down
there remains

approximate
to the distance halved
forever ending

the sky above
off tune

slightly

7

out of another time
another mouth moving
inside this one

say "I" once more
and the door will shut
forever

"but who can live
wordless" asks the vole

step away from the mirror
remove those reading glasses
you've become all too human
the words want to claim us
as their own

stop shaking
and draw the silver string
from your animal eye
to the evergreen in the distance

perhaps I have failed you
in anthropomorphic oversight

or am I not listening
close enough

8

I know you must
hear the inevitable crunch
of little teeth in the background

getting closer

the sun and stars never appear
in the same breath

but now you see them
crossing

is this the buried sky

the world eating itself
word by word

or simply language

stretched over everything
in a sticky embrace

9

the one who lives
in terminal stutter

the correction to all
and every last

conviction come to this

words will fail us in the end
I have no doubt

corporeal weightlessness
in the tremor
night terrors
riding on the whim
of a changing wind

pivot on a pronoun
that turns away
from the finished sentence

that we might listen in
to the silence thick
as air and waiting

deaf to your voice
I hear my own unspoken
at the imaginary
doubling of this world

connect the dots
and a bear waddles across the sky
lose the thread and the stars
return as facts

between the sound and its echo
enough distance to dream

only in separation do we seem
to cross and in crossing
divide

little tremble
sit beside me

in the vast and cloistered

a vole buried in the earth
the earth buried in space

as words would have it
the sentence bends both ways

DEAD RECKONING V

Objects Release Their Frozen Stare

1

love may pass through the eye of death
I don't know it's a tight squeeze

it's everything and nothing all rolled into one
you can think anything you want

most do and end up
in their own back pocket

(little squeak of truth there)
but when nobody really needs you

they can't really care
and when that goes on year after year

you may find yourself squeezing through
the butterfly valves of your own heart

2

lights fade and the stars begin to bloom
wild flowers in the skull

dreams are not just dreams
anymore than a hand is just a hand

or a shovel is just a . . . tool
everything is itself and something else

sounds like you and me
shadowing this afterbirth they call real life

the ones living it never meet
the ghosts inside them

or maybe it's the ghosts that fall in love
and existence just goes along for the ride

3

start with the surrounds the shimmering abyss
between you and the chair

this region of apparitions this nothing
around everything which is never quite empty

my blue hands for instance
swimming in space are starting to disappear

it's a trick of the eye I have no doubt
something akin to the background swallowing

the foreground or the object taking it's revenge
in the half-light I see a large saint bernard

has risen from behind the couch and is pressing
a paw to my jugular checking for a pulse

4

my animals come to me
in a trickle of trance notes

I send them raining down your window
always open to a play on words

but this time you weren't listening
to the tiny thoroughbred racing across your temples

instead your body drove a buick
face first into a tree and all the names

and places disappeared on your palm
your thighs poured in at the hip

mountains bent as my lips slipped
under radar to find you

5

will come a time a name
plucked from pregnant air

when the headless woman walks through me
into the open sea

luminous thread drawn through a needle
as the eye in sleep travels

retina-stitch through the fabric of this world
humming across the same discontinuous

outline in the mirror the same
stranger's face I take for my own

the one already dead and the other who
cannot die are kissing cousins in the glass

6

as I talk to you someone talks to me
little reversals under the shell of an accident

ghosts inside the minds of others
I am what haunts and what is haunted

but is absent at its core
without a clear beginning or end

perhaps this space between us this life
suspended in the void was a place

only visited in dreams
but we knew how to get there

the present is always a little dead my dear
we are already living in the afterlife

About the Author

Charles Borkhuis' six previous collections of poems include: *Afterimage* (Chax Press 2006), *Savoir-fear* (Meeting Eyes Bindery/ Spuyten Duyvil 2003), and *Alpha Ruins* (Bucknell University Press-2000), selected by Fanny Howe as a finalist for the William Carlos Williams Book Award. His poems have been anthologized in *An Avec Sampler #2* (Avec 1998), *Primary Trouble* (Talisman House 1996), and *Writing From The New Coast: Presentation and Technique* (o.blek 12 1993). His essays on contemporary poetics have appeared in two books from the University of Alabama Press: *Telling it Slant* (2000) and *We Who Love to Be Astonished* (2002*).* Borkhuis' work has appeared in numerous journals including: *American Letters and Commentary, Avec, Big Bridge, Eoagh, First Intensity, Five Fingers, Jacket, New American Writing, o.blek, Ribot, Second Avenue Poetry, Skanky Possum, Talisman, Van Gogh's Ear, Verse,* and *The World.* He curated poetry readings for the Segue Foundation in NYC for 15 years. He translated *New Exercises* by Franck André Jamme (Wave 2008). The author of over 35 plays, his work has been presented in New York, Hartford, Los Angeles, Paris, and San Francisco. His plays have been published in *Mouth of Shadows* (Spuyten Duyvil 2000), *The Sound of Fear Clapping* (Obscure Press 2003), and *Present Tense* (Stage This 3 2009). His two radio plays, *Foreign Bodies* and *The Sound of Fear Clapping* were produced for NPR (www.pennsound). He is the recipient of a Dramalogue Award and is the former editor of Theater:Ex (1986-1988), an experimental theater publication. His recent NY productions include: *Present Tense* (Alchemical Theater Lab. 2013), *Barely There*, and *Flipper* (Harvestworks 2013). He lives in New York City and has taught at Touro College and Hofstra University.

About Chax Press

Chax Press is a 501(c)(3) nonprofit organization, founded in 1984, and has published more than 140 books, including fine art and trade editions of literature and book arts works.

For more information, please see our web site at http://chax.org

Chax Press is supported by individual contributions, and by the Tucson Pima Art Council and the Arizona Commision on the Arts, with funds from the State of Arizona and the National Endowment for the Arts.